Original title:
Frosted Ravens

Author: Lan Donne
ISBN HARDBACK: 978-9908-52-491-7
ISBN PAPERBACK: 978-9908-52-492-4
ISBN EBOOK: 978-9908-52-493-1

## The Icy Veil of Solitude

Beneath the stars, the world is bright,
Whispers of joy in the frosty night.
Crystals shimmer on branches bare,
A festive spirit dances in the air.

With laughter ringing, hearts unite,
From shadowed corners, a warm delight.
Flakes of wonder drift from above,
Wrapped in warmth, we share our love.

## Clarity Beneath the Glacial Sky

Under the glacial sky, so vast and clear,
We gather together, our loved ones near.
The air is crisp, filled with hope and cheer,
In this festive moment, the world feels dear.

Stars twinkle brightly, a jubilant cheer,
Illuminating faces with joy sincere.
With every heartbeat, connections flow,
Beneath the glacial sky, our spirits glow.

# Frosted Whispers at Dawn

The morning glows with frosty light,
Snowflakes dance in joyful flight,
Laughter echoes, hearts so warm,
In this magic, we transform.

Glistening paths of purest white,
Children play with pure delight,
Cocoa cups and fireside cheer,
Together we bring the year near.

Sparkling lights on every tree,
Whispers of joy, so wild and free,
Songs of winter fill the air,
In this moment, love we share.

Every breath a cloud of mist,
In this festive, tranquil tryst,
As dawn breaks, our spirits soar,
In frozen realms, forevermore.

## Echoes of Shadows on Chilly Reverie

Beneath the stars, a chill in the night,
Festive laughter, hearts feeling light,
Shadowy whispers, secrets to share,
In the crisp air, love lingers there.

Glowing lanterns, soft and bright,
Guide us through the frosty flight,
Carols sung with voices high,
In every note, our spirits fly.

Chill in the air, but warmth in our souls,
Gathered together, we fill the roles,
Memories woven like treasures dear,
In this chilly reverie, we hold near.

Toast to the night with cheer and glee,
Surrounded by friends, joyous company,
Echoes of shadows dance and sway,
In this festive night, we find our way.

## Midnight Wings of Winter's Breath

In the glow of twilight's gleam,
Snowflakes dance, a silver dream.
Beneath the stars, the world aglow,
Joyful hearts, where laughter flows.

Mirthful spirits fill the air,
With every snowflake, pure and rare.
As carolers sing of peace and cheer,
Together we gather, holding dear.

## Shadows Wrapped in Silver

The moonlight bathes the world in grace,
Whispers of magic in every space.
Dancing shadows sway with delight,
As winter's spirit ignites the night.

Bright lights twinkle on every tree,
Filling our hearts with warmth and glee.
Stories shared around the flame,
In this moment, we're all the same.

## Echoes of the Icebound Sky

Beneath the vast, enchanting dome,
Voices mingle, now far from home.
Every laugh, an echo so sweet,
As we gather where joy and magic meet.

A tapestry woven with bonds so tight,
In the glow of festivities, our hearts take flight.
With every clink of glass in cheer,
We toast to the warmth that this season brings near.

## Whispers Beneath the Crystal Canopy

Under branches draped in frost,
We celebrate, forgetting the cost.
Laughter sparkles in the air,
Absorbing joy, we release our care.

The night is young, and so are we,
In every heartbeat, pure harmony.
With winter's breath upon our cheeks,
We find the magic that each heart seeks.

# Traces of Dusk on Crystal Fields

As day's last light begins to fade,
The crystal fields in twilight laid.
Whispers dance on winter's breath,
In festive hues, they tease of death.

Beneath the stars that twinkle bright,
Frolic shadows in the night.
Joyful hearts in frosty air,
Cherish moments, free from care.

With laughter ringing through the vale,
A spark of warmth within the pale.
Each footstep crunches on the frost,
In this wonderland, we never lost.

So let us feast beneath the glow,
Of twinkling lights and falling snow.
In crystal realms where dreams may soar,
A night of joy we can't ignore.

# Moonlit Shadows in a Frosted Slumber

Beneath the moon's enchanting gaze,
The world adorned in icy blaze.
Shadowed whispers, soft and low,
In winter's grip, warm hearts still glow.

Each flake that falls, a silvered note,
A choir of laughter, dreams remote.
We gather close, in cozy cheer,
Our spirits bright throughout the year.

The frost-kissed air, a gentle thrill,
Invites us all to pause and chill.
With every breath, we share a smile,
In frosted realms, let's linger awhile.

Let's clutch our mugs of spiced delight,
And cherish every winter night.
In moonlit shadows, we find our song,
A festive heart where we belong.

# Winged Reverie on Icy Trails

On icy trails where omens fly,
Bright-winged dreams in winter's sky.
Fires of joy in every glance,
We skip along this frozen dance.

The air is thick with laughter's cheer,
As whispers of the night draw near.
In patterns etched by fleeting light,
We revel here, beneath the night.

Snowflakes twirl like playful sprites,
Carving paths through starry nights.
Together weaving tales to share,
In every breath, a promise there.

So let us fly on wings of dreams,
Through frosted lands where magic gleams.
In harmony, our voices blend,
A festive spirit that won't end.

# Black Feathers Beneath a White Canopy

In winter's realm, both stark and bold,
Where black feathers dance, their stories told.
Beneath a white canopy, pure and bright,
Festive spirits roam through the night.

The crispness of the air ignites,
A spark of joy in frosty bites.
With every step, the echoes ring,
Of playful hearts and flapping wing.

Each feather drifts on gentle breeze,
Carving paths through snow-drenched trees.
With laughter mixed within the chill,
A vibrant thrill, our souls fulfill.

So gather close as fires glow,
In black and white, the warmth we sow.
In nature's quilt, together we stand,
Creating magic, hand in hand.

## Sable Silhouettes in White

Under stars, the shadows dance,
In the night, we find our chance.
Ribbons bright and laughter soar,
With every cheer, we ask for more.

Frosty breath in the crisp air,
Glowing lights in festive flair.
Sable tales of joy we weave,
In this moment, we believe.

Joyful voices fill the night,
Guided by the moon's soft light.
Whispers sweet, the snowflakes glide,
In this magic, we abide.

Embrace the warmth, let worries cease,
In the silence, find our peace.
Sable silhouettes take flight,
In the heart of pure delight.

## Beneath the Crystalline Canopy

Underneath a shimmering sky,
Dreams in crystals hover high.
Hanging lights like stars appear,
Laughter echoes, brings us near.

Festive wishes on the breeze,
Drifting gently through the trees.
Every branch adorned in grace,
In this chill, we find our place.

Beneath the glow of winter's breath,
We gather close, defying death.
Mirth and joy, our hearts ignite,
In the dance of this sweet night.

Sipping cocoa, sweet delight,
As merry voices spark the white.
Beneath a crystalline embrace,
Together, we find our space.

# Murmurs of a Frigid Dawn

In the dawn, the whispers play,
Chilling winds that sway and sway.
Frosted branches, soft and round,
A new day born in silence found.

Glistening hues of pink and gold,
Tales of warmth begin unfold.
As ice and fire meet in dance,
We embrace the fleeting chance.

Murmurs soft beneath the sky,
Promises as fleeting as a sigh.
With every breath, we let it go,
In the chill, our spirits glow.

A frigid dawn, yet hearts are warm,
In every storm, we weather calm.
Together we share this frosty fawn,
In the magic of the dawn.

## Shards of Light on Midnight Wings

On midnight wings, the lights do soar,
Shards of magic at our door.
With every flicker, dreams take flight,
In the dark, we find our light.

Silhouettes of joy in sway,
Gather close and laugh away.
In this canvas, shadows twine,
Every moment feels divine.

Whispers sweet in air so light,
Sparkling stars, a glorious sight.
In the rhythm of the night,
Hearts entwined in pure delight.

Celebrate the twinkling dream,
Every smile, a love supreme.
Shards of light above us gleam,
In this magic, we all beam.

# A Sable Song on a Winter's Breath


Whispers dance in the frosty air,
Candles flicker, warmth we share.
Laughter mingles with the snow,
Hearts aglow in the evening's flow.

Joyful carols fill the night,
Stars above twinkle bright.
Mittens clasped, we stroll around,
In this bliss, our love is found.

The cocoa steams, sweet delight,
As we gather in the light.
Fire crackles, embers glow,
In this moment, time moves slow.

Together we craft, hearts entwined,
A sable song, forever aligned.
As winter wraps us in its cheer,
Each breath shared, a warm frontier.

## Twilight Trails on Frozen Paths

Under the twilight's gentle grace,
Footsteps echo, a merry pace.
Snowflakes glisten, soft and light,
As laughter soars, a pure delight.

Fires crackle, tales unfold,
Bundled snug in vibrant gold.
In every sip of spiced cheer,
Memories woven, season's dear.

Glistening trees, adorned so bright,
Guiding us through the starry night.
With every breath, a joyous song,
Together we wander, where hearts belong.

On frozen paths, we dance and sway,
In the glow of the festive display.
Holding hands, we face the chill,
In the warmth of love, we find our fill.

# Echoes of the Chilling Vale

In the vale where echoes play,
Winter's breath leads the way.
Footprints trail upon the snow,
Guide us where the soft winds blow.

Bells ring out with a hearty cheer,
Celebrations drawing near.
Under blankets, stories shared,
In the hearth's glow, love declared.

Stars reflect on frozen streams,
As we weave our cozy dreams.
Crunch of snow beneath our feet,
In this dance, our hearts compete.

With every laugh, the chill subsides,
In the echoes, warmth abides.
Together we rise, never frail,
In this winter, joy prevails.

## Serene Shadows in Frosty Shelters

In frosty shelters, shadows play,
Secrets whispered, soft and gay.
Through the glass, the world aglow,
A tapestry of white below.

Mistletoe hung, kisses shared,
In the quiet, love declared.
While outside, the cold winds blow,
Inside, warmth begins to grow.

Candied fruits and spiced delight,
Fill our hearts with purest light.
Songs of joy, we sing in tune,
Beneath the gaze of a silver moon.

In serene shadows, we find peace,
Every moment, joy will increase.
Together in this frosty embrace,
Our hearts aligned, a timeless space.

## Veils of the Winter Wind

Snowflakes twirl and dance so bright,
Wrapping the world in purest white.
Laughter echoes in the air,
Joyful hearts devoid of care.

Candles flicker, warm their glow,
Radiant smiles in the falling snow.
With every toast and cheer we raise,
We celebrate through frosty days.

# A Dance of Cold and Shadow

Under the moon's soft silver sheen,
Whispers of joy, crisp and clean.
Footprints trace the snow's cold bed,
In shadows long, where dreams are spread.

Gathered close, we share our tales,
Through nights adorned with snowflakes' veils.
With every smile, warmth does lend,
A dance of shadows, hearts to blend.

# The Muted Call of the Chill

Chill winds sing a muted song,
As laughter weaves where we belong.
Fires crackle, warmth ignites,
Hearts aglow on winter nights.

With cocoa cups and marshmallows sweet,
Friends gather round, a festive treat.
In quiet moments, joy unfolds,
The muted call of winter holds.

# Embracing Winter's Veil

Winter's veil, a soft embrace,
Encircles us in its gentle grace.
With every spark the fire casts,
Together old and new amassed.

Carols sung with voices clear,
Fill the night with festive cheer.
While snowflakes kiss the earth below,
We celebrate in winter's glow.

# Strands of Ice and Night

Underneath the starry night,
Strands of ice gleam with delight.
Laughter dances through the air,
Festive spirits everywhere.

Twinkling lights adorn the trees,
Whispers carried by the breeze.
Joyful songs and playful cheer,
Winter's magic draws us near.

Children play in frosty dreams,
Sipping cocoa, sweetened creams.
Every heart is warm with light,
In this festive, wondrous night.

Glittering like jewels bright,
Strands of ice in soft moonlight.
Let's embrace the joy we share,
In this season, love and care.

## Chilled Prowess of Shadows

Shadows dance in frosty glow,
As the cold winds start to blow.
Laughter echoes through the streets,
Festive joy in every beat.

Chilled prowess of the night air,
Spins a tale without a care.
Merriment within the throng,
Hearts united in a song.

Candles flicker, warmth they send,
As the joyful moments blend.
Wisps of laughter intertwine,
In this tapestry divine.

Gather close, both young and old,
Sharing stories oft retold.
Chilled prowess we embrace,
In the festive night's embrace.

# Whispers of Winter's Wings

Whispers soft as winter's wings,
Carried on the breeze, it sings.
Sparkling flakes twirl in delight,
Creating visions pure and bright.

Gathered 'round the fireside glow,
Tales of wonder start to flow.
Joy and laughter fill the air,
Festive warmth beyond compare.

Beneath the moon's gentle light,
Friends unite, and hearts feel bright.
In this moment let us soar,
Whispers of winter, forevermore.

Embrace the night, let joy ring,
In the magic that we bring.
Let our voices raise and blend,
In this season that won't end.

# Shadows Drenched in Ice

Shadows drenched in crystals freeze,
Whispers flow upon the breeze.
Festive wonders all around,
In this winter, joy is found.

Glistening paths where we tread,
Sparkling dreams in silver thread.
Every heart with warmth ignites,
In the glow of starry nights.

So gather close, hear laughter ring,
In the warmth that friendship brings.
Shadows dance, and spirits glide,
In this festive, joyful ride.

Through the night, our voices rise,
Drenched in ice, we claim the skies.
With cheer and love, we'll embrace,
Every moment, every place.

# Wings Adrift in a Frozen Dream

Dancing lights swirl in the night,
Whispers of joy take their flight.
Laughter echoes through the trees,
As stars twinkle in the breeze.

Snowflakes twirl in a gleeful swirl,
Festive magic all around.
Families gather, flags unfurl,
In this wonderland, we're spellbound.

Warm cocoa steams in bright hands,
Tales of miracles unfold.
Gentle hearts make cozy plans,
As dreams of peace begin to mold.

Wings adrift on winter's air,
Spirits soaring, bold and free.
In this moment, free from care,
A frozen dream for all to see.

## Feathered Shadows at Dusk

As the sun begins to set,
Feathered shadows softly flit.
Candles glow with warm embrace,
Lighting up each joyful face.

Carols drift on whispered winds,
Unite the hearts that winter sends.
Harmonies fill the colorful sky,
As magic weaves, and spirits fly.

Gathered close, the stories told,
Echoing in the night so bold.
Feathered friends take to their nest,
Under the stars, we feel so blessed.

The dusk invites us to partake,
In love and laughter, we awake.
Time slows down, a gentle hush,
In feathered shadows, we find our rush.

# The Enigma of Winter's Embrace

A blanket of white covers the ground,
Underneath, whispers can be found.
The chill carries songs of the past,
With frozen smiles, the die is cast.

Twinkling lights give secrets away,
Glistening dreams in the frosty gray.
Each corner echoes with joyous cheer,
In winter's embrace, all hearts draw near.

Moments of wonder shaped like snow,
As laughter dances, it starts to glow.
Warmth of the fire, a soothing sight,
As we wrap ourselves in pure delight.

The enigma unfolds, like frosty breath,
Life's simple joys, defying death.
Together we weave this glorious tale,
In winter's embrace, we will prevail.

# Ashen Plumes in the Cold

The world adorned in silver hue,
Ashen plumes rise, fresh and new.
Whispers of warmth in frosty air,
Hearts entwined in love and care.

Glimmers of hope blink in the night,
Children laugh at pure delight.
Each snowball thrown, a joy we share,
In this cold, warmth is everywhere.

Finding treasure in frozen streams,
Chasing echoes of childhood dreams.
Hot cider warms our willing hands,
As we celebrate in festive bands.

Ashen plumes swirl, dancing high,
Under the vast, enchanting sky.
Together we bask in this magical glow,
In winter's wonder, our spirits grow.

# Wings Cloaked in Frosty Silence

Beneath the stars, the night is bright,
Soft whispers dance, of pure delight.
Feathers glide with graceful ease,
In the chill, they swirl like leaves.

Laughter echoes, spirits high,
With every flake, a joyful sigh.
Hearts aglow in frosty air,
Magic woven, everywhere.

The world adorned in silver lace,
With every turn, a warm embrace.
Glimmers shine in whispered light,
A festivity that feels so right.

Together we soar through the night,
On frosty wings, our dreams take flight.
With joy and peace, our souls unite,
In this serene and wondrous sight.

# The Glistening Abyss

In the depths where secrets play,
Glitters dance, in bright array.
Bubbles rise, like laughter's call,
While starlit shadows gently fall.

Every sparkle tells a tale,
Of secret worlds where dreams set sail.
Joyful echoes, pure and sweet,
In this abyss, where wishes meet.

The glistening waves, a festive cheer,
Inviting all, come, gather near.
Beneath the surface, life abounds,
In laughter's depths, true joy resounds.

Together we bask in the glow,
Where every breath ignites the flow.
In this realm of wondrous play,
The glistening abyss lights our way.

# Moonlight's Icy Embrace

A blanket of silver, soft and bright,
Cocooned in dreams by the moon's light.
Frosted whispers on winter's breath,
Dancing shadows, a joyful quest.

With every beam, the world transforms,
Creating magic in hidden forms.
In this embrace, our worries fade,
In moonlit glow, joy is displayed.

Stars twinkle like playful sprites,
Guiding hearts on snowy nights.
With laughter filled, the spirits rise,
In this embrace, a grand surprise.

Together we twirl on icy ground,
As midnight's charm in silence found.
In moonlight's arms, our hearts race free,
A festive night, just you and me.

# Frost-Kissed Flight

With frosty wings, the world unfolds,
A canvas bright with silver golds.
Each gentle lift, a thrill to share,
As dreams take flight in crisp night air.

Glistening paths beneath our feet,
Sparkling joys that feel so sweet.
With every glide, our hearts align,
In festive cheer, our spirits shine.

Through woven paths of winter's chill,
We chase the stars with vibrant will.
Together soaring, hand in hand,
In frosty flight, we take our stand.

Let laughter ring and echoes roar,
With frost-kissed dreams, we all explore.
In joyful swoops, and leaps so grand,
We're bound in night, our dreams unplanned.

# The Lament of Shivering Feathers

In the dance of twilight's glow,
Feathers flutter, dreams in tow.
Whispers soft on chilling air,
Joy and sorrow weave a pair.

Laughter rings through chilly nights,
Candles flicker, hearts take flight.
Underneath the starry dome,
Feathers find their way back home.

Each flake falls like whispered song,
Echoes bright where all belong.
With every gust, new tales unfold,
A festive warmth against the cold.

So let the shivering cease today,
As colors dance in grand array.
For in this mirth we find our place,
Feathers aloft in joy's embrace.

## Silent Watchers of the Snow

Beneath white drapes of purest calm,
Silent watchers weave their charm.
Branches heavy, cloaked in light,
A festive hush cloaks the night.

Nestled close, the world now waits,
Nature's pause and gentle fates.
Snowflakes twirl like little stars,
While laughter echoes near and far.

In this quiet, joy takes flight,
Illuminated by the night.
Each flake lands with magic's grace,
A winter's tale in a still space.

Silent watchers, oh so wise,
Keep the secrets of the skies.
In their gaze, we find the cheer,
To warm our hearts as winter nears.

### Ethereal Melodies of the Frozen Realm

A symphony in frosty air,
Ethereal tunes dance without care.
Nature's music, soft and sweet,
Invites us to rise to our feet.

Crystal chimes from icicles sway,
Melodies weave through winter play.
With each note, the shadows shift,
A festive spirit, a precious gift.

Frosty bushes, glistening bright,
Echo the joy in the night.
Whispers of laughter, crisp and clear,
Encircle all who gather near.

In this realm of frozen dreams,
Life unfolds in silver beams.
Let the melodies fill the air,
In every heart, a vibrant flair.

## The Gaze of Winter's Guardians

Amid the snow, the guardians stand,
Watching over this frozen land.
With eyes that shimmer, wise and old,
They cradle tales of warmth untold.

In every flake, their gaze is found,
A festive cheer that knows no bound.
Against the chill, they share a spark,
Guiding all through the cheerfully dark.

Bundles wrapped in love's embrace,
Light up the night, a warm trace.
With laughter bright, they light the way,
Guardians of joy on this winter's day.

So let us gather, spirits high,
Beneath the watch of the starry sky.
Together we soar, hearts entwined,
In the gaze of guardians, love defined.

# The Shivering Silhouette

In the glow of lanterns bright,
Laughter dances through the night.
Colors twinkle, spirits rise,
Joy reflected in our eyes.

Snowflakes twirl like cotton dreams,
Gliding softly on moonbeams.
Voices mingle, hearts align,
In this festivity, we shine.

Around the warmth of crackling fire,
We share stories that inspire.
Glimmers of hope in every cheer,
In this moment, love draws near.

As the evening drifts away,
We hold these memories to stay.
Together, in the winter's light,
We savor magic, pure delight.

## Night's Claw in the Snow

Beneath the starry, frosty veil,
Voices rise like a joyous gale.
Each footstep crunches fresh and clear,
Echoing laughter, spreading cheer.

Twinkling lights adorn the trees,
Carols flow on the gentle breeze.
Gathered close, friends hand in hand,
Creating memories, oh so grand.

In the embrace of winter's hold,
Stories of wonder we retold.
With every smile and playful jest,
The chill fades, we are truly blessed.

As blissful moments weave their tune,
Hearts ignite like the brightening moon.
In this beauty, warm and true,
The festive spirit lives in you.

# A Chill's Embrace at Dusk

As daylight wanes and shadows grow,
The world is wrapped in a silvery glow.
Laughter echoes through the trees,
Carried lightly by the breeze.

Candles flicker, casting light,
On this wondrous winter night.
Friends gather close, their voices high,
In the dance of joy, we'll amplify.

Glasses raised, a toast to cheer,
We celebrate love with those we hold dear.
Songs of hope fill the air,
In this circle, we laugh, we care.

Beneath the sky, we find our space,
A chill's embrace, but warmth we trace.
In every heart, the spirit sways,
As we revel in these festive days.

# Frostbound Wings in a Whispering Wood

In the forest where whispers play,
Snowflakes flutter, drift away.
Branches glisten, diamonds bright,
Nature's canvas, pure delight.

Children giggle, spirits soar,
Building dreams on winter's floor.
Every snowman, every ball,
Wrapped in laughter, we enthrall.

As night falls, we gather near,
Tales of wonder, joy, and cheer.
Underneath the starlit skies,
Each heart dances, love never denies.

With frostbound wings, we take to flight,
Through this wonderland of light.
In this magic, forever will stay,
The festive spirit leads our way.

# The Shivering Call of Dusk

As daylight fades, the colors glow,
A party spirit starts to flow.
With laughter ringing through the night,
We gather 'round, hearts feeling light.

The stars above begin to dance,
In a festive mood, we take a chance.
To sing and share our joyful cheers,
And toast to love that steers our years.

The twilight whispers tales of old,
While stories spark like embers' gold.
We savor treats, both sweet and bright,
As evening deepens, hearts take flight.

With every clink of glass we cheer,
For friends and joy we hold so dear.
Together, we embrace the night,
As dusk unfolds its blanket, tight.

# Raven's Lament in Winter's Grip

The raven calls through zephyr's chill,
In winter's touch, the world stands still.
Yet beneath the frost, life plays a tune,
As hearts grow warm by the light of the moon.

With candles glowing, spirits soar,
We gather close, we seek for more.
In whispered tales of laughter shared,
The chill resolves, as joy is bared.

The snowflakes twirl like dancers bright,
We celebrate this magical night.
With every step, we glide and sway,
The winter's chill can't steal our play.

So let the raven's song resound,
In frosty fields, let joy abound.
Despite the cold, our hearts will glow,
In festive warmth through wind and snow.

# Frosted Whispers Beneath the Stars

Beneath the stars, the world twinkles bright,
Frosted whispers weave through the night.
With laughter shared and stories spun,
Each moment feasts, for joy's begun.

The frosty air is filled with cheer,
As friends and kin all gather near.
We sip on cocoa, sweet and warm,
In this festive night, we weather charm.

With every spark, our spirits gleam,
We dance and sing, igniting a dream.
The moonlight casts a silver hue,
As we twirl beneath the skies so blue.

Each frosted whisper, each glint of light,
Holds secrets of a joyful night.
Together bound, hearts intertwined,
A timeless bond, forever enshrined.

# A Symphony of Icy Echoes

In the stillness of the spectral night,
Icy echoes ring with pure delight.
With every sparkle, the world ignites,
A symphony of laughter takes flight.

Beneath the trees, the shadows sway,
We gather 'round, let magic play.
With songs that linger in the air,
We craft our dreams, we shed all care.

The chilly breeze brings festive cheer,
As joy resounds, we hold it near.
With every flash from lanterns bright,
We chase away the cloak of night.

So clap in rhythm, let voices blend,
In the icy grip, our hearts extend.
We celebrate the bonds we weave,
In a symphony of love, we believe.

# Beneath the Glacial Veil

Beneath the glacial veil we dance,
With laughter bright in winter's trance.
Sparkling snowflakes gently fall,
As joyous voices rise and call.

The air is crisp, the sky so blue,
With friends and warmth, our spirits grew.
A glow of light in every heart,
In this cold world, we play our part.

Twinkling lights adorn the trees,
As whispers of the night-time breeze.
Come join the chorus, sing out loud,
In winter's magic, we are proud.

So raise a glass, let laughter soar,
In this embrace, we ask for more.
Beneath the glacial veil, we sway,
In festive cheer, we live today.

## Dark Beaks and Shimmering Stars

Under twilight's gentle touch,
Crows gather in their playful clutch.
With dark beaks gleaming, they take flight,
Beneath the stars, our hearts feel light.

The night sky drapes in deep embrace,
As laughter joins the starry space.
We share our stories, dreams untold,
In festive whispers, brave and bold.

The crows above, a dance of grace,
As we unite, time slows its pace.
With every chuckle, joy ignites,
Beneath the glow of twinkling lights.

So let the night unfold its charm,
In each warm hug, we find our calm.
Dark beaks and shimmering stars align,
In this embrace, our hearts entwine.

# Entwined in the Cold Night

Entwined in the cold night's embrace,
We gather here, a merry place.
With frosty breath and laughter sweet,
The joy of friendship, pure and neat.

A circle formed, we share tales grand,
With every smile, we take a stand.
The moon above shines bright on us,
In winter's hold, it's magical trust.

Snowflakes twirl, a whimsical sight,
As we dance in the crisp twilight.
Hot cocoa flows, with marshmallows bright,
Tonight the world feels just so right.

So let the chill breeze be our song,
In festive cheer, we all belong.
Entwined in warmth, we raise a cheer,
For every moment, held so dear.

## Crows Adorned in Frost

Crows adorned in frost take flight,
Against the canvas of the night.
With wings spread wide, they dance with glee,
In the festive air, so wild and free.

We gather round a fire's glow,
Sharing secrets only we know.
With laughter ringing, spirits soar,
In this cold, our hearts explore.

The stars above twinkle like dreams,
As we toast to life and all it seems.
With every moment, warmth ignites,
In the embrace of winter nights.

Crows take flight, a joyful tease,
In their frosty world, our hearts appease.
Let's dance along, with spirits so bold,
In this festive season, let tales unfold.

# In the Stillness of Icy Veils

Beneath the twinkling stars we sway,
Laughter dances in the chill of night,
A tapestry of dreams on display,
Joyful hearts shining, pure delight.

Snowflakes whisper secrets untold,
Glistening in the moon's gentle light,
Warmth in our spirits, unfurling bold,
Together we celebrate, feeling right.

Candles flicker in frosty embrace,
Songs of the ancients fill the air,
In this moment, time leaves no trace,
Magic and wonder everywhere.

Gathered around the fire's warm glow,
We weave stories wrapped in delight,
In the stillness, let our hearts show,
Unified in joy, we take flight.

## The Dusk Where Shadows Gathered

The sun dips low in vibrant hues,
Colors merging, painting the sky,
As laughter echoes, a joyous muse,
Children's delight, let spirits fly.

Lights aglow in the gathering dark,
Glimmers of warmth in the cooling air,
Each heartbeat a soft, radiant spark,
Moments of bliss, we gladly share.

Songs intertwined with the crisp, cool breeze,
Whispers of love in the fading light,
Festive spirits dance with such ease,
Inviting all to join the night.

Beneath the stars, we raise our cheer,
In the dusk where shadows convene,
Together we laugh, forgetting our fear,
In this embrace, we are serene.

# Elegy of the Frostbitten Sky

In winter's breath, a melody rare,
With holly and ivy adorning the hall,
Life sparkles like frost in the crisp night air,
An elegy sung, joyous and tall.

Chiming bells beckon, a festive delight,
Fields of silver stretch wide and free,
Under the heavens, stars shining bright,
Our hearts beat as one in sweet harmony.

Gifts wrapped in laughter, stories unfold,
Each moment cherished, a treasure divine,
Candles reflecting memories of old,
Together we toast as the stars align.

Celebrate life in this frosty embrace,
For in the chill, warmth always resides,
In the elegance of the night's gentle grace,
We find our joy where happiness abides.

# The Frost Within the Flight

On wings of laughter, we soar so high,
Through snow-kissed clouds, our spirits glide,
With hearts alight, we embrace the sky,
In the bright expanse, joy cannot hide.

The frosty air carries tunes of the past,
Echoes of cheer from days gone by,
In every whisper, our dreams are cast,
Upward we rise, allowing us to fly.

Stars twinkle softly, a guiding light,
Bathed in a glow of a festive cheer,
Finding enchantment in the frosty night,
Our laughter blends with the crystal clear.

Let us dance among the flakes that fall,
Each one a wish, a dream set free,
In the essence of flight, we heed the call,
Together forever, in harmony.

# The Chill of Darkened Feathers

In the night, the lanterns glow,
Whispers of joy begin to flow,
Around the fire, laughter rings,
As magic in the cold air clings.

Snowflakes dance on winter breeze,
Hearts are light, they're filled with ease,
Together we shall sing tonight,
Underneath the stars so bright.

With cloaks of velvet, soft and warm,
We gather close, away from harm,
In this embrace, peace takes its flight,
As shadows flicker, all feels right.

Let the chill weave through the air,
In every heart, there's warmth to share,
As hands entwined, we greet the night,
In the chill of darkened light.

## Frozen Ebon Dreams

Beneath the sky, a silver sheen,
Our wishes float like stars unseen,
In frozen ebon, dreams take flight,
We gather hearts, we share the light.

Winter's breath, a gentle tease,
With every touch, a magic freeze,
Hope ignites in whispered songs,
As night envelops, it rightes wrongs.

Fire crackles, shadows dance,
Moments given, a fleeting chance,
Through frosted glass, we see the past,
But in this night, our bonds hold fast.

Embrace the frost, the dreams it brings,
In every glance, a joy that sings,
Together we create our scheme,
In the beauty of frozen dreams.

# Twilight's Shimmering Shadows

As twilight falls, the world aglow,
With shimmering shadows, hearts bestow,
Under the stars, we find our way,
And let our spirits dance and sway.

In the crisp air, laughter wakes,
A melody of joy it makes,
Candles flicker, bright and bold,
Stories shared, both new and old.

The night unfolds with every cheer,
Embracing dreams held close and dear,
In this place, our troubles cease,
We wrap ourselves in warmth of peace.

From dusk till dawn, let feelings soar,
In every heart, we keep a score,
With twilight's shimmer, we'll ignite,
A celebration through the night.

## Song of the Frostbitten Night

The frostbitten night, a glorious spree,
Wrapped in warmth, just you and me,
With every note the world inspired,
A melody of joy, we're wired.

Candles burn with flickering grace,
Reflecting dreams upon each face,
Through snowy fields, our laughter streams,
With every breath, we chase our dreams.

Dancing shadows waltz and play,
In our hearts, the music stays,
A tapestry of voices bright,
Together, we embrace the night.

And as the stars ignite the sky,
In unity, we laugh and sigh,
The song of frost, our spirits light,
In the beauty of this night so bright.

## Plumes Against a Winter Canvas

Snowflakes dance in the bright moonlight,
Colors twirl in festive delight.
Whispers of joy in the crisp, cold air,
Laughter echoes, a song we share.

Pine trees dressed in silver and gold,
Stories of warmth in the winter's cold.
Children play under starlit skies,
With every twirl, the spirit flies.

A feast laid out with love and cheer,
Friends gather close, the season near.
Toasting with glasses, sparkling bright,
A celebration under the night.

As dawn breaks softly, the colors show,
Winter's canvas, a lovely glow.
With hearts aglow, we embrace the thrill,
In this festive moment, time stands still.

# Twilight's Icebound Messengers

Crystals shimmer in the fading light,
Twilight beckons, the world is bright.
Greeting the night with a frosty spin,
Joyful echoes, where dreams begin.

Fires crackle with tales untold,
Gathered 'round, we let warmth unfold.
The air is filled with laughter and song,
As icebound messengers come along.

Glowing lanterns, a path to trace,
In every heart, a joyful space.
With every step, we twirl and glide,
Under the stars, we take our stride.

A kinship formed through the winter's breath,
Celebrating life, defying death.
Twilight wraps us in a festive thrill,
As we dance together, time stands still.

## Winter's Heralds of Darkness

Night descends with a magical hue,
The world transformed, fresh and new.
Candles flicker, casting warm light,
Winter's heralds bring forth the night.

Snowmen rise, adorned with charm,
In this stillness, we find our calm.
With every smile, the darkness fades,
As joy and laughter in us cascades.

Carols sung in the crisp, clear air,
Voices rising, a song to share.
With family near, hearts feel the glow,
In winter's embrace, our spirits flow.

The trees are dressed in diamonds bright,
A wondrous sight, pure and white.
By firelight's warmth, our spirits soar,
In winter's magic, we find much more.

# Elegy for the Venomous Chill

As frost bites deep, we stand so bold,
With hearts aflame, and stories told.
An elegy sings to the chill at bay,
Yet winter's grace leads us to play.

The air is sharp, but joy remains,
In every laugh, the spirit gains.
Snowflakes swirl like soft confetti,
Nature's party, a dance so ready.

We bundle close, our hearts unite,
In shared warmth, we find our light.
As chill retreats, we raise a cheer,
Embracing the season, holding it dear.

Through winter's bite, we'll find our way,
With every moment, our spirits sway.
An elegy for chill, with each spark ignites,
The festive spirit, our hearts delight.

# Shadows Played in Frigid Light

In the glow of twilight's gleam,
Snowflakes twirl, a dancing dream,
Colors shimmer, laughter bright,
Shadows played in frigid light.

Bells ring clear, a joyful sound,
Whispers of the night abound,
Frosty air, so crisp and mild,
Magic sparkles, hearts beguiled.

Glistening trails where footsteps tread,
By the fire, where tales are spread,
Mirthful spirits take their flight,
In the shadows, pure delight.

Christmas cheer, a warm embrace,
Live in joy, let sorrow face,
Underneath the starry sight,
Shadows played in frigid light.

# The Dance of Ice at Night

Underneath the silver moon,
Chill winds sing a frosty tune,
Stars will twinkle, bright and bold,
The dance of ice, a story told.

Whirling dancers, soft and slow,
Gliding on the sheets below,
Every twirl enchants the air,
Winter's wonder everywhere.

Children laugh, their spirits free,
Chasing dreams in jubilee,
Twinkling lights, a warm delight,
The dance of ice, pure and bright.

A chorus of the night's delight,
Echoing through the starry night,
Join us now, take flight anew,
Feel the magic, fresh and true.

# A Glance from the Icy Abyss

Glimmers shine from frosty deep,
Secrets long in slumbers sleep,
Whispers ride on snowy breeze,
A glance from the icy abyss, please.

Shadows dart through crystal clear,
Frozen laughter warms the sphere,
Nature's art, a splendid sight,
Glimping dreams in cold moonlight.

Mysteries within the frost,
Adventures found, never lost,
Stars align in the chilly night,
A glance from the icy abyss, excite.

Gather 'round let spirits soar,
Feel the thrill and so much more,
In this realm of pure twilight,
A glance from the icy abyss, bright.

## Winter's Winged Secrets Revealed

Snowflakes dance like whispered tales,
Along the path where laughter hails,
Underneath the satin sky,
Winter's winged secrets, oh my!

Feathers drift on frozen air,
Winging journeys without care,
In the hush, soft voices blend,
Warm our hearts, let magic mend.

Joyous songs in frosty breath,
Celebrate the dance of death,
With each flutter, dreams are sealed,
Winter's winged secrets revealed.

Gather close, let spirits sing,
Feel the joy that heartbeats bring,
Magic spins with every thrill,
In winter's realm, time stands still.

# The Lament of Winter Colors

Amidst the gray, a flicker bright,
Crimson leaves take their flight,
Joy wrapped in a golden glow,
As winter weaves its final bow.

In twilight's arms, we gather near,
Candles glimmer, hearts feel cheer,
A feast of laughter fills the air,
With every smile, the cold we dare.

Branches bare, yet spirits high,
Underneath the darkened sky,
In every flame, a tale ignites,
A tapestry of winter nights.

So let us dance, let voices swell,
In every joy, winter's spell,
With colors bright and hearts aglow,
A festive song for all to know.

# Whispers in the Frigid Air

Beneath the stars, the silence sighs,
Whispers drift from winter skies,
Frosted breath and laughter shared,
In every glance, the warmth declared.

Carols rise on crisp moonlight,
Bringing joy, a pure delight,
Hands held close, our spirits soar,
In the cold, we find much more.

Snowflakes fall, a gentle grace,
Painting smiles on every face,
We gather 'round the flickering flame,
In winter's heart, we feel the same.

So come together, let's embrace,
The magic that this night can trace,
For every breath, a story shared,
In whispers soft, love is declared.

# Specters in the Powdered Snow

Underneath the pale moon's glow,
Footsteps dance in fresh soft snow,
With every crunch, a story spun,
The season's spirit has begun.

Silhouettes of joy in white,
Laughter echoes through the night,
Snowmen stand with playful grins,
As the festive magic begins.

Fires crackle, hot cocoa flows,
Warm embraces, spirit grows,
In the chill, our hearts ignite,
With winter's charm, the world feels right.

So lift your glass, let joy resound,
In this dance, our love is found,
For in the frost, the world transforms,
A celebration, our hearts adorn.

# The Stillness of Hoarfrost Wings

In stillness lies the magic's kiss,
Hoarfrost wings in a winter's bliss,
Dreams take flight on the chilly breeze,
Whispers carried through frosted trees.

A tapestry of white unfurls,
In every glassy crystal swirls,
With every sigh, a tale takes form,
As festive hearts begin to warm.

Gather 'round the sparkling glow,
Feasts await, the spirits flow,
Bright colors dance on every plate,
United we stand, together, fate.

So let our voices rise and blend,
In winter's arms, together mend,
With hoarfrost wings, we dare to sing,
In joyous hearts, the warmth we bring.

## Shadows Among the Ice

Beneath the sparkling stars so bright,
The shadows dance in pure delight.
Whispers of laughter fill the night,
With joy that glows, a festive sight.

Ice crystals twinkle on the ground,
As merry voices swirl around.
In every heart, a warmth is found,
In this embrace, true bliss is crowned.

Colors glimmer, bright and bold,
Stories shared, both young and old.
In this magic, we unfold,
Together, memories to hold.

So let the music play and rise,
With every beat, our spirits fly.
In shadows sweet, the world collides,
In midnight joy, our laughter ties.

## The Gleam of Midnight Wings

Under the moon, where dreams take flight,
Midnight wings sway in pure delight.
The air is filled with songs so bright,
A festive spirit paints the night.

Each flutter glows like stardust fair,
Dancing softly through the cold air.
With twinkling lights and joyful flair,
Together, joy we freely share.

Firelight flickers, shadows play,
As whispers of hope shout, 'Hooray!'
In every heart, a song will stay,
In the chill, warmth shall not sway.

Embrace the moment, let it sing,
In laughter loud, our souls take wing.
Through every note, let love take ring,
In the gleam, each memory spring.

# Haunting Notes in a Frozen Air

In the hush, where silence reigns,
Haunting notes drift through the plains.
Winter's chill, yet warmth sustains,
In every heart, the joy remains.

The stories told by glowing flame,
In frozen air, we call your name.
With every laugh, we stake our claim,
Together wrapped, in festive fame.

Symphonies of nature's call,
Dance like shadows at the hall.
With every rise, let's heed the thrall,
In winter's grip, we find our all.

So take my hand, let's roam and play,
Through snowy nights that twirl and sway.
In the haunting notes, we find our way,
In frozen realms, the heart's ballet.

## The Stillness of the Winter Watch

In the stillness where whispers freeze,
Winter watches with gentle ease.
Under the stars, a moment's seize,
As spirits rise on the frosty breeze.

Branches laced with crystals fair,
Reflect the glow of soft moon's glare.
In every pause, a love laid bare,
Festive songs linger in the air.

Gathered close, our hearts entwined,
In this stillness, warmth we find.
Through laughter shared and spirits kind,
In winter's arms, our souls aligned.

So let the night enfold us tight,
With every star, our dreams take flight.
In the stillness that feels so right,
May joy and love be our delight.

# The Whispering Wings of Solstice

In the glow of festive lights,
Joy dances in the air,
Every heart feels the delight,
As laughter weaves everywhere.

Snowflakes twirl like little dreams,
Painting white on all we see,
Children play by silent streams,
Gleeful shouts of pure esprit.

Candles flicker, shadows sway,
Songs of warmth fill every space,
Hope ignites this wondrous day,
As we gather, each embrace.

With every whispered wing in flight,
The solstice calls us to rejoice,
In the magic of the night,
Together, we all find our voice.

## Nightfall's Frosted Songbirds

Underneath the silver moon,
Softly chirp the songbirds bright,
Their tunes create a gentle rune,
Guiding us through wintry night.

Frosted branches sway with cheer,
Each note dances in the breeze,
Voices ringing, crystal clear,
Nature sings as hearts find ease.

Families gather, stories share,
With mugs of warmth in their hands,
Laughter echoes, fills the air,
As we build our joyful lands.

Nightfall wraps us in its song,
As songbirds flutter, swift and free,
In this festivity so strong,
Together, we feel harmony.

## Beneath the Frosted Canopy

Beneath the trees in glistening white,
We gather 'round with spirits high,
The frost creating pure delight,
As dreams of joy begin to fly.

Candles glow, and shadows play,
The canopy whispers tales of old,
Magic woven in every way,
A festive night for hearts so bold.

Children's laughter fills the air,
Snowmen stand with grins so wide,
The joy of winter everywhere,
In this wonder, we abide.

Under twinkling stars above,
Every moment holds a spark,
In this place of peace and love,
Our voices blend, a gentle lark.

# Sable Wings in a Snowy Exile

Sable wings glide through the night,
Seeking warmth in a frosted land,
With every flap, a twinkling light,
In the stillness, joy expands.

The snowflakes twirl in soft ballet,
While laughter echoes through the trees,
Each whisper brings a bright array,
Of hope that dances in the breeze.

Gathered friends, we share our cheer,
As stories weave from heart to heart,
In this moment, pure and clear,
We embrace winter's gentle art.

Though nights may linger, cold and long,
The warmth of kinship lights our flame,
Together we sing a timeless song,
In snowy exile, love's the same.

## Mysterious Shadows on a Frosty Eave

Whispers of night in the frosty air,
Shadows flit softly, secrets to share.
Twinkling stars drape the eaves in light,
A dance of the shadows, a festive sight.

Laughter echoes, the crispness sings,
Frost-kissed branches, the joy winter brings.
Glimmers of warmth in a cold, bright night,
Hearts full of wonder, spirits take flight.

## The Stark Beauty of Frozen Heights

Snow-capped peaks in the silver glow,
Nature's artwork, a winter show.
The world seems still, yet alive with cheer,
Frozen wonders, the beauty is clear.

Crystals sparkle like diamonds bright,
Hope and joy dance in the cold moonlight.
A celebration in every heart's beat,
In frozen heights, the world feels complete.

## Black Feathers among Snowflakes

Feathers drift gently, a soft, dark hue,
Against the pure white of the snow's fresh view.
A contrast bold, a festive delight,
Winter's canvas, a magical sight.

Echoes of laughter, the children play,
In a world of wonder, they twirl and sway.
The dance of the snowflakes, a joy to behold,
In shadows of black, a story unfolds.

## Midnight Dancers in Icy Air

Under the moon, a chill in the breeze,
Figures whirl and twirl with elegant ease.
Dressed in the shimmer of frost and night,
Midnight dancers bring warmth, pure delight.

The air is electric, the stars twinkle bright,
As laughter and music take airy flight.
A festival's spirit, alive in each heart,
In icy embrace, we never shall part.

# Cinders of a Winter's Night

Flickering flames dance in the night,
Warmth spreads smiles, hearts take flight.
Laughter rings through the chilly air,
Together we weave, a bond so rare.

Beneath the stars, we gather close,
In the warmth of friendship, we rejoice.
Cinders glow, memories ignite,
Celebrating life, a pure delight.

Snowflakes twirl in joyful play,
Dreams take shape, come what may.
With every toast, we share our dreams,
Under the moonlight, love redeems.

Hearts are full as the night grows late,
Finding magic in every fate.
Cinders fade, but spirits rise,
In winter's embrace, pure delight lies.

# Frosted Veils in Twilight

Beneath the frost, the world shines bright,
Veils of silver in fading light.
Whispers of joy fill the crisp air,
Harmonies dance in a moment rare.

Glimmers of hope as day gives way,
The twilight wraps us in its play.
Laughter echoes, warmth in sight,
Together we bask in the fading light.

Candles glow in a dazzling array,
Softening shadows where we lay.
Every smile is a twinkling star,
Drawing us closer, no matter how far.

With hearts aglow in festive cheer,
We hold each other, drawing near.
Frosted tales under the dark blue sky,
In these moments, together we fly.

## Crystalized Murmurs of the Shadows

In the stillness, whispers flow,
Crystalized secrets, a soft glow.
Shadows dance like spirits bold,
Embracing stories yet untold.

Each shimmering laugh a vibrant hue,
Painting the night with memories new.
As music swells, we sway in time,
Lost in the rhythm, a joyful chime.

Glistening dreams sail through the dark,
Arising hopes, igniting a spark.
In the shadows, we find our light,
The magic lies, oh, what a sight!

Crafting a tapestry, bright as day,
With every heartbeat, come what may.
Crystalized murmurs float in our hearts,
Binding us close, never to part.

# Chilling Echoes of the Deep

In the quiet depths, there's a song,
Chilling echoes where we belong.
With every note, a memory stirs,
Binding us in laughter, joy, and purrs.

Underneath the starlit dome,
We find our place, we feel at home.
Together we weave a tale so grand,
In the cooling mist, we hold hands.

Flickering lights in the distant waves,
Call to our spirits, their song saves.
Through the darkness, our dreams take flight,
Chasing the echoes, igniting the night.

As the ocean hums beneath the sky,
We share our hopes, no need to shy.
In the chilling whispers of the deep,
We forge our bond, a treasure to keep.